DALLINGTON HALL

1720–2020

BY

MARINA OLIVER

Marina Oliver

Dallington Hall 1720-2020

Published by Marina Oliver

See details of other books by Marina Oliver at
www.marina-oliver.net
www.sally-james.net

ISBN 9780244239923

Dedicated to the hundreds of people who have lived or worked at Dallington Hall

FOREWORD

I have to thank the many people who helped in this project.

My husband Chris found maps.
My daughter Jackie Stopyra combed through newspaper archives.
My daughter Debbie guided me through census records on Ancestry.co.uk
Mervyn Bridges gave me documents and pictures.
I was also much indebted to his booklet on the church.
Marjorie Cook lent me documents relating to the Almshouses.
Peter Bateman gave me a guided tour of the Tennis Club.
Christine Musson's booklet on the village houses was invaluable.
Helen Clarke gave me photographs.
Gaynor Chute helped explore Record Office documents.
The Golf Club at Great Harrowden Hall lent me a book on the house's history, including the Sharpe School.
The National Portrait Gallery gave me permission to reproduce portraits of Sir Richard Rainsford (sic) and Sir Joseph Jekyll.
Grace's Guide to British Industry gave me permission to reproduce the picture of the Lewis Brothers' Factory.

INTRODUCTION

Dallington Hall, sometimes known as Court, or House, has been a private house, a boarding school, a convalescent home, and divided into eleven apartments. For much of the time, even before this house was built, the manor of Dallington was associated with parliamentarians.

Initially this project was intended to be a history of the house, three hundred years old in 2020, but in the way of these things it expanded to cover the village and the manor too. As such a small village it has had a surprising amount of national importance through the owners of the manor.

There are two villages named Dallington. The other is in East Sussex, and also a small place. The Oxford Names Dictionary refers to the Sussex one as 'an estate associated with a man called Dalla', and cites it as Old English, but there is no entry for Dalla in either the surname or first name sections, or for us specifically in the place names.

In this sort of research there are inevitably many unanswered questions, so there are many 'possiblys' and 'probablys', speculation about the most likely but unproven answers.

NORTHAMPTON AND DALLINGTON

Dallington, a mile and a half to the west of Northampton, is now a part of the county town but always had close links to it, especially as the town spread westwards. The west gate was the town's major entrance.

This close connection was made easy by the major route of the present Harlestone Road, which diverged from the Roman road, now the A5, at Stony Stratford, came through Northampton and Dallington, on to Leicester and Derby and eventually to Manchester. It was probably one of the post roads set up in Tudor times to help royal and government messengers have easy passage, and made available in the seventeenth century to other carriers of private letters. In 1783 there is a mention of the first Earl's body, after his death, being brought home and passing through the town to the Dallington Gate. In 1878 the Turnpike Trusts were dissolved and a new County Council took over road maintenance.

For Northampton there are references to Roman

and Anglo Saxon remains. Several ancient remains have been found to the north west of Spencer bridge, on the outskirts of Dallington village. As well as mammoth tusks there have been worked and polished flints from the Bronze Age, arrow heads, Iron Age and Roman pottery and a Cunobelinus coin. The Cymbeline in Shakespeare's play, ruling over south-east Britain, he died in AD 42. To the north of Dallington village crop marks, evidence of enclosures and a causeway have been found as well as Roman coins and a possible Roman settlement.

The town became important only under the Danes, who made it a centre around 900. In 918 Edward (The Elder, a son of Alfred the Great) reconquered it and it became the focus for a new shire, but was still being fought over by the Danes and British. In 1010 it is called a 'port', a trading place. In 1086 it contained about 316 houses, and was in between Warwick and Leicester in size. Leicester had 322 houses in 1066 and a population of between 1500-2,000, while Warwick was slightly smaller.

There were also several religious houses, more than in other nearby towns. As well as the Cluniac priory at Delapré Abbey, there were Graye Friars, Blackfriars and Whitefriars, plus St James' Abbey in Dallington. The latter held a big fair on St James' day, July 25th, and after the dissolution this remained as a town fair until the beginning of the eighteenth century.

After the Norman conquest and in medieval times Northampton became an important strategical point being in the centre of England, on the road north from London. It was surrounded by deer forests and the River Nene, which was then a salmon river, connected with the sea. The castle, built in 1084, was taken over as a royal residence and fortress. Many meetings, including parliaments, were held there, the last parliament being in 1380, after which the town declined in importance. During the civil war in the seventeenth century Northampton was for Parliament, and it had strong Puritan and non-conformist traditions.

The markets and fairs were major events. Dallington, so close, could have benefited from this as people arrived. At the edge of Dallington, near the town, was the Abbey of St James, an Augustinian monastery founded in 1104 with endowments in Duston. It quickly became rich and influential. An annual fair was granted to St James in 1268, held at St James' End beyond the town's west bridge. The Abbey had an infirmary, and a burial ground in which many people asked to be buried. It was dissolved in 1538 and the borough held its lease lands known as the Duston lordship.

Northamptonshire was one of the major sheep breeding counties, so enclosures of the old field system came early. In 1720 the lordship of Dallington was enclosed by private agreement, with forty acres allocated to the Vicarage, and eight to St James, the rest to the owner of the manor. The big open fields surrounding Dallington were enclosed and in 1820 also the common fields. In 1765 and 1776 Kingsthorpe and Duston fields were also enclosed.

For many centuries shoe-making in the town and some surrounding villages has been a major industry, and still flourishes.

In 1914 part of Dallington was added to the Northampton civil parish, and in 1931 the remaining parish was split. Dallington fell from 1,520 acres to 842, with a population of more than 5,000, while Duston with

686 acres had a population of 36.

DALLINGTON VILLAGE

There was an Anglo Saxon settlement at Dallington, and the remains of a Saxon church were discovered. However, the most reliable evidence is 1086 Domesday. The village then belonged to Peterborough Abbey, when Abbot Thorold, in 1069, distributed land to several stipendiary knights to get aid against Hereward the Wake. Dallington came to a Norman knight called Richard. The manor extends from the edge of the town, along Harlestone Road to Harlestone Heath, and back along the Nene valley.

The soil varies from clay in the east to light sand in the north and north east. Later, in the north, 150 acres were planted with beech and fir with ridings. There was arable land enough for eight ploughs, two of which were in the demesne, ie land for the private use of the lord of the manor that was not let out. Each plough could till about 120 acres, enough to support a family for a year. These measurements, which varied in different parts of the country, were used for taxation assessments by the Normans.

According to the Domesday survey in 1086 there were 18 villeins, a priest, and four bordars, ie villeins who held cottages at the lord's pleasure. In 1220 a Rector came to the village. This implies there was by then a church.

There was a mill with five acres of meadow down by what is now Spencer Bridge Road. Under Edward the Confessor it had been worth 40 shillings a year, but under the Normans this was increased to 100 shillings. The water power for the mill came from Dallington Brook, which ran beside what is now Dallington Road and into the Naseby branch of the Nene. The three ponds, the lowest of which is now in the tennis club grounds, are thought to be medieval, though they had been changed in more recent times, probably after 1720, and with the Brook have sluices dating from the eighteenth and nineteenth century. In March 1855 the Royal Humane Society awarded a medal to Dallington Hall butler, Thomas Wadd, who, 'under circumstances of great difficulty', saved the life of a boy who had fallen into the water whilst skating on one of the ponds.

In 1801 the village population was 302, in 60 houses. By 1841 there were 509 residents. In 1841 were a corn miller, two victuallers, a beer retailer, baker, blacksmith, maltster, two shopkeepers, a carpenter and farmers.

In 1911, the last publicly available census, there were 65 houses and the population was 268. In that year the oak tree on the Green was planted to commemorate the coronation of George V. In 1932, after the building of the Spencer estate, there were 360 people in the old parish and 6,000 altogether. The population at St James' End had incrcased a great deal, many working in the shoe factories.

Memorial Tree Planted 1911

It is interesting to

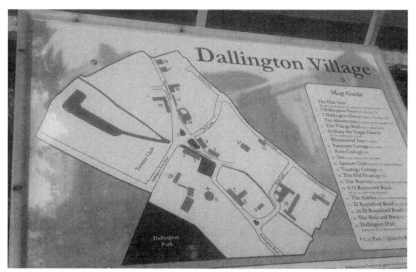

Houses in Conservation Area

compare the 1851 and 1911 census records. The quality of the first detailed census in 1841 is too poor to be useful, but in 1851 there were 112 men, 42 of them described as agricultural labourers, and three farmers. There were seventeen shoemakers, and eleven servants. In 1911 the range of occupations is far more varied, but there were five farmers and four dairy farmers, though some of these men belonged to the same families and were probably not operating separate businesses. There were fewer labourers, though some were more specific as dairyman, waggoner, cowman, and two gamekeepers. Interestingly, there were also eight described as market gardeners. There were still seventeen shoemakers.

By now there were also more 'gentry' - a retired surgeon, solicitor, brewery owner, two brewery managers, architect, coal and coke merchant, timber and builders' merchant, and an insurance branch manager. As a consequence there were also more servants, nineteen compared with eleven. There were also more dressmakers (ten instead of one), six 'domestic' gardeners, a coachman, nursemaid, and a laundress.

In 1932 the village became part of Northampton borough. In January 1970 10.3 acres of the older part of the village was designated a conservation area.

ST MARY THE VIRGIN

The church of St Mary the Virgin was built between 1207 and 1252, erected on the remains of the decayed Saxon church. A piece of sandstone with carved figures in the north wall may  be a piece of a Saxon cross. This suggests the north aisle was the first to be built. As with most churches stone seats, still visible, were provided for the aged and infirm, while the rest of the congregation stood. A low window in the south wall is unexplained. It could be a leper window or for confession, even for a bell to be rung during Mass.

There have been many recent changes, such as re-roofing and new windows. A partial rebuilding of the south aisle in 1877 uncovered a piscina, which implied there had once been an altar there. More windows were inserted at this time. Part of the tower was rebuilt in 1863, and the chancel extended in 1883. At this time a screen (reredos) was erected behind the altar.

It is the typical layout of nave, two aisles, and chancel, with a tower to the west and a south porch. The Raynsford mortuary chapel, now a vestry, was built during the seventeenth century, and there are family memorials, including several windows. A lengthy Latin inscription extols Sir Richard Raynsford's virtues. His wife Dame Catherine presented a large flagon to the church in 1698. Both the Raynsford and Jekyll families supported the church with gifts.

The advowson (right to present a vicar) passed to the Corbets after the dissolution. In later years several Jekylls were Vicars of Dallington. There is a mural monument to one of the Jekylls and Lady Anne Jekyll presented a salver. The Rev Richard Blackett Jekyll, who was Vicar until 1752 (probably since 1739 when the previous vicar resigned) gave a chalice and patten in 1752. An organ was presented in about 1883 by Mrs H.B.Whitworth of Dallington Hall. An alms dish was presented in 1906 in memory of Margaret, Viscountess Althorp.

In 1741 a new vicarage was built on ground obtained from Joseph Jekyll (Sir Joseph's nephew) in exchange for the site of the old vicarage, then in ruins. The Rector Fiennes Samuel Trotman added a new dining room to accommodate his large family, but it was removed by a later Rector. He also planted on the lawn a cedar which had come from Lebanon.

The next Vicar, Christopher Cookson, did much to restore the church, often at his own expense. He founded the daughter parish of St James' which was opened in 1869. He also started the harvest festival celebrations. After him came Thomas Beasley, who had the last of the 'horse-box' pews removed.

DALLINGTON HALL

The demesne land attached to Dallington Hall was a long plot between Dallington Road and Harlestone Road, running from what is now Warren Road towards Dallington Heath. There was farmland to the north-west of the three lakes.

The house is described thus:

'1720-30 for Sir Joseph Jekyll, Master of the Rolls. Symmetrical design in ashlar. Hipped tiled roof behind low parapet and cornice. 2 storeys, basement and attics. Entrance front has Doric end pilasters under entablatures with triglyphs and guttae, 5 sash windows with glazing bars in eared architrave surrounds under keystones. 3 gabled dormers. Central doorway up steps has 8-panelled door and rectangular fanlight in architrave surround under pediment on consoles. Garden front

similar but with 7 windows, central 3 on 1st floor roundheaded between tall pilasters. Pedimented central doorway. Interior: panelled staircase well, close string stairs with twisted turned balusters, carved spandrels.'

There is no evidence as to an architect. But Francis Smith, of a Warwick family of builders and contractors, worked on numerous houses and churches throughout the Midlands, including Lamport, and probably Great Harrowden Hall. The latter, also built about 1720, is very similar in design to Dallington, and its staircase, built by Warwick men Joseph Daniel and Daniel Wyman, who were employed by John Smith of Warwick, almost identical.

The large front door opened into a hall that occupied the north-east corner of the ground floor. To the right were a large front room and two smaller ones behind. Behind the hall was a passageway with the main staircase on the right and a secondary staircase to the left, with a small room in between.

The elegant main staircase and the rest of the house are now Grade 2*. This staircase, with shallow and wide steps, was used during the days of the convalescent home to help patients learn how to climb stairs again. The other staircase led from the basement past the main and bedroom floors to the attics. These would have accommodated the servants and at times a nursery. Each half landing on these stairs extended into a bay overlooking the back garden.

The basement would have been kitchens and quarters for the servants, and there appears to have been a dumb waiter lift from the kitchens to the hall, which was probably used for dining.

It is thought the lower Dower House extension was added fairly soon after the main house was built, so that the entrance hall lost the two side windows. The windows at the front are very slightly different from those in the original house. At first the roof sloped down against the wall of the main house, but later was extended so that there was access at that level.

It could have been a 'granny flat', or more likely meant to add more living space, since it was just one

room deep, and probably just two rooms with a basement and attic. It enclosed a courtyard at the back, edged by the boundary wall of the church, and adjoining the stable yard, and from it a two-storey passageway, probably built much later, led to the gatehouse and the buildings in the stable yard.

The stables were older than the house, being built in the seventeenth century. There would have been a coach house, now the largest of the courtyard houses, which may later have been a barn or a farmhouse. There is evidence of buildings backing onto the passageway from the house, protruding further than the existing garages. These would probably have been a tack room and feed stores, and maybe stables.

In the wall adjacent to the churchyard there seems to have been a large entrance, now bricked up. Permission to convert the stables into houses and build garages was granted in 1999. There were more stables and other buildings in another yard now occupied by a house, Stable Cottage, and a narrow passageway connecting the two yards.

When the Hall was bought by the Spencers in 1863 it was described as having fifteen bedrooms, but it is difficult to reconstruct their layout. There were extensive stabling and coach houses, laundry, brewhouse, flower gardens and pleasure grounds. When the house became a convalescent home the stables were converted to accommodation.

In 1950 planning permission was given for the construction of a bed lift at the side of the house, beside the secondary staircase. This lift was larger than normal to accommodate the beds or trolleys of the convalescent home. More rooms were added later on each floor to the far side of the lift. This took up about half of the inner courtyard.

By 1977 the home was under threat of closure. It was by then a pre-convalescent unit of Northampton General hospital. It had 32 part time staff and 30 beds.

It is rumoured that there are three ghosts, a little boy (from which period is not known, but presumably later than 1720 unless he was a remnant of the earlier manor house), a soldier (similarly of unknown origin) and the Matron of the convalescent home which occupied the Hall between the two world wars. She is reputed to walk from the main house, where women patients were installed, along the two-storey passageway to the men's wards in the stable yard.

Today there is a path leading down from the front garden to what had been the kitchen courtyard. Part of the old kitchens had to be demolished to allow access, and traces of an old fireplace are visible. It was probably constructed when the house was converted to apartments. Previously deliveries to the kitchens and access for servants would have been via the stable yard.

THE GARDENS

There was a path round the perimeter of the garden, hoggin from which was unearthed when a flower border was made against the wall dividing the garden from the churchyard. There is a door in this wall, now unused, from the back garden to the churchyard.

When the house was converted to apartments part of the south east section of this long site, behind the house, was sold and houses built on the land. This part of the demesne was described, in the auction particulars of 1863, as two walled gardens, with vinery, conservatory, forcing pits, and a productive orchard.

To the front of the house the grounds stretched on the far side of Dallington Park Road, which was little more than a muddy track, through what is now the Tennis Club. This was established in 1886, the land rented by agreement with Earl Spencer, and which included the lakes. The upper, largest lake, once had a bathing pool, a punt and diving platform, and many fish including carp. In winter it made a good skating lake.

When Mill Lane was constructed in 1980, forming a road to Kingsthorpe where previously had been just a very muddy path beyond King's Heath, it cut the club premises in two, and eventually the furthest part was rented to a fishing club. There are badgers now in both halves of the plot, and an access tunnel originally built for the tennis club users.

In the corner of the tennis club, as Dallington Park Road turns to become Raynsford Road, there was once an

ice house, to which ice was brought from the big lake. There was also a very tall dove cote, and a well that had to be filled in when a new tennis court was built. Water was pumped via pipes.

In March 1877 there was an agreement between the fifth Earl and tenant Henry Billington Whitworth, a Northampton banker, to occupy the Hall and a gardener's cottage, with gardens, orchard, stabling and so on. The landlord had to organise and keep in repair the pumps that brought water from the ponds to the house. Mr Whitworth died six months later and his widow remained at the Hall for some years.

In the late nineteenth century Dallington Park and some farm land were sold. In earlier times what is now the Park had been two large fields, Upper and Middle Warren. This is where rabbits, hares and partridges were raised. In the early nineteenth century the ha-ha wall and ditch separating the Park from the house gardens were built, probably because the warren was no longer used and instead sheep grazed in these fields.

The large house on the corner of Dallington Park Road and the Harlestone Road was built in 1882, and others further along Harlestone Road at about the same time. Several plots adjacent to Harlestone Road to the north west were sold off. The houses on the NW side of Dallington Park Road were built in the mid twentieth century. Various conditions were

Going home from milking

imposed on their uses. Previously there had been a farm, from which the cows had walked to the dairy near the Vicarage each day to be milked.

INHERITANCE CHAIN

According to a lecture Samuel Sharpe, of Dallington Hall, gave in 1864, the following people owned the manor. It is noticeable how many daughters inherited. Finally, the manor was sold rather than inherited.

Robert de Frehlle

daughter = Eustace de Broc

daughter Eva = Walter Kineto de Chesni of Slapton

Amabil = Almaric Despencer (1193)

(He held 2 knights' fees, but Eva de Broc claimed against him, as his only right came from Walter, who gave it with his daughter Amabil)

Juliana = Geoffrey de Lucy

son (1207)

(de Lucy family had much property elsewhere)

9 generations of de Lucy 1207-1460

3 of the Barons were Barons of Parliament

Last de Lucy, William, killed at the Battle of Northampton. Had no sons, but two sisters

Matilda = Lord Vaux of Harrowden

Elizabeth = (2) John Tiptoft, Earl of Worcester. An outstanding scholar, also known as a 'butcher'. Beheaded 1470 by Lancastrians

= (3) Sir William Stanley of Holt. He saved life of Henry VII at Bosworth. Later he was accused of complicity with Warbeck, and beheaded 1495, Henry seized possessions

Elizabeth = Corbutt (Corbet). Family held Dallington for 16 generations until daughter

Elizabeth = Sir Henry Wallop, MP, of Farley, Hants

Sir Robert Wallop (Parliamentarian). One of judges at trial of Charles I, but did not sign death warrant. At Restoration dragged on sledge to Tyburn and back to Tower.

He sold Dallington to

Richard Raynsford of Staverton before civil war. Knighted 1663. Chief Justice in 1676

Son

Daughter Anne = James, 2nd Lord Griffin

Son & 2 daughters who inherited Dallington &
1720 sold it to

Joseph Jekyll

great-nephew Joseph = Anne, daughter of Earl of
Halifax. Died 1752

Anne = George Wrighte of Gayhurst. He died 1804

Daughter Anne Barbara Wrighte, born 1784, died
unmarried 1828, left it to

Miss Sarah Newsham = John Reddall in 1832

Anne Wrighte asked her friend Sarah Newsham, a
clergyman's daughter, to live with her. In 1811 the butler
and maid were charged in the Aylesbury court with theft.
For six years he had taken wine to London to sell when
he wanted cash, while the maid, with Miss Wrighte for
over twenty years, helped herself to whatever she wanted.
An apothecary who had been made steward assisted
them. When noises were heard during the night, and
masked men approached the ladies in the domain Park,
they were forced to leave the house. They went to live in
Sidmouth, south Devon.

Sarah was connected to the Trotman family. She
died in 1848 and left Dallington to her husband for life,
and when he died in 1856, to her brother in law, the
vicar Feinnes Samuel Trotman. He immediately rented
the property out to the school run by the Sharpes. He in
turn died in Jan/Feb 1863, and the property was sold in
June that year. An earlier attempt to sell in 1850 failed.
The Sharpes announced in 1864 that their lease had
been renewed. The Spencer family, having bought
Dallington, now owned land stretching from Althorp to
the town.

THE RAYNSFORDS

The Raynsford family had old royal and parliamentary connections. A Sir John Raynsford served both Henry VII and Henry VIII. His son was a member of parliament in 1529. The family originated in Essex, but some of them moved about. A John Raynsford who died circa 1500 lived at Rainsford (the spelling varied frequently) Hall in Lancashire. His descendants and ancestors appear to be the same family as Henry Rainsford, born about 1410, who lived in Oxfordshire, probably at Great Tew. His descendants lived in Essex and came eventually to Staverton, round about 1600.

Sir Richard Raynsford was born at Staverton in 1605, the second son of Robert and his second wife Mary Kirton, of Thorpe Mandeville in Northamptonshire. He studied at Oxford but left without graduating. This was not unusual. As a student at Lincoln's Inn he was elected Recorder of Daventry in 1630, and called to the bar in 1632. In 1653 he was made Recorder of Northampton. In 1660 at the restoration of Charles II Richard Raynsford was elected to the national

Sir Richard Rainsford after Gilbert Soest
©National Portrait Gallery, London

convention, and again in 1661 and 1662 to Parliament as a member for Northampton, until he was raised to the Bench in 1663 as Baron of the Exchequer. In 1676 he became Chief Justice of the King's Bench. He was President of the Court of Claims in Ireland, and as such is mentioned in Samuel Pepys' Diary in 1664. He died in 1680.

He married Catherine, daughter of Rev Samuel Clerke, Rector at St Peter's, Northampton, at Kingsthorpe in 1637. They lived in the Manor House at Dallington. She died in 1698. They had five daughters and six sons, but most died young. His eldest son Richard (II) became MP for Northampton in 1685, and died in 1702/3.

His daughter Anne, married to James, the second Lord Griffin, had a son and two daughters, the latter inheriting Dallington. Elizabeth married Henry Neville Grey of Billingweare in Berkshire, while Anne married William Whitwell of Oundle.

Another son, Edward, emigrated to America with the Pilgrim Fathers, and settled on Rainsford Island in Boston Harbour. This was at different times a quarantine hospital, unmarked burial ground for the diseased and criminals, almshouse, veterans' hospital, reform school, and resort.

ALMSHOUSES

Sir Richard built the almshouses on the village green in 1673, for four poor people, preferably two men and two women. The silver badges meant to be worn by the inhabitants when at church are preserved with the church plate. They had two shillings (10 pence) each every week, money which came from the rent of

£27/14/0 on property in St Saviour's, Southwark, and had to wear at all times a garment of cloth or baize, a new one given them each year.

A plaque, in Latin, gives the date of the founding, the 29th of September 1673, by Sir Richard Raynsford, and concludes 'Let none dare to violate them. Vengeance is God's.'

In 1701 his son, another Richard, appointed the trustees. In 1819 Joseph Jekyll Rye became one of the trustees, Richard Jekyll Rye having given property by his will.

The name was changed, and later, in 1897 when Joseph Shuttleworth, the brewery owner, gave £100 in celebration of Victoria's Jubilee, his name was added to the official Almshouse name, the Raynsford, Rye & Shuttleworth.

This money was invested in shares and the profits distributed every Whitsun. Later, another Mr Shuttleworth was involved in building the houses on the NW side of Dallington Park Road, and increased their number from the original five which had been permitted.

When Mr Morgan was Vicar, 1947-60, he had the almshouses rebuilt and added bathrooms and inside toilets. His successor, Mr Pyburn, with ten men of the parish, moved 80 tons of stone from Old Lodge Farm, given by Northampton Corporation, for a 2'6" wall to be built in front of the almshouses and school. Paving stones were added later.

Mr Richard Croft was Chairman of the Parish Council in 1896, and was one of the trustees. In 1927 Mr T.D.Lewis was appointed a trustee. Mr Lewis, a shoe manufacturer, and his brothers bought Dallington Park for the borough of Northampton.

VILLAGE SCHOOL

In 1840, with grants from the National Society, the schoolroom next to the Almshouses was built. In 1911 there were a Head Teacher, an Assistant, and a School Monitor. In 1924 it had 93 pupils, some from Duston, but in August 1939 was closed. The room was bought in 1961 by the Church Council for £100 for use as a village hall.

SIR JOSEPH JEKYLL

The Dallington Manor was sold by the Raynsford family to Sir Joseph Jekyll, and he began building the new house in 1720, on the site of the old one. This was not Sir

Joseph's main residence, which was at Brookmans in Hertfordshire. He probably spent very little time at either house, since he would need to be in London when Parliament was sitting, usually for at least six months each year. He came from a large family, having twelve siblings and numerous nieces and nephews, though he himself had no children. Several Jekylls were associated with Dallington later, so perhaps he built the Hall for their use. He was, it was said, generous to his relations.

The four cottages on the Green, facing the almshouses, were also built in 1720, perhaps for estate

servants. The end one became a smithy. As this year, especially in the first six months, was an extremely busy one in Parliament, with problems of the South Sea Company, it is probable that building did not start until later that year. Besides, the old manor house had to be demolished first, and some of the rubble was used in the stable yard. This had previously been taxed on fifteen hearths, quite a large building.

Sir Joseph was born in 1663 to John Jekyll, of a family originating in Lincolnshire. His father was a

S. *JOSEPH JEKYLL Knight,* *MASTER of the ROLLS.*

Sir Joseph Jekyll by George Vertue ©
National Portrait Gallery, London

fishmonger and Alderman of St Stephen's Walbrook. He was the seventh son. He attended a Nonconformist seminary in Islington until, in 1680, he joined the Middle Temple and was called to the Bar in 1687. He was Chief Justice of Chester in 1697, and in the same year became a Whig Member of Parliament for Eye in Suffolk at a by-election. He was knighted that year.

In 1713 he became MP for Lymington, and in 1722 for Reigate. He became Master of the Rolls in 1717. This was the second most important judicial appointment, and involved keeping the government records, which used to be written up on 'rolls' of parchment.

He was described as having a hatchet face and surly look, and always looked grave and spoke sententiously. Several painters did portraits of him.

In about 1690 he married Lady Elizabeth Somers, born 1655, the younger sister of the Lord Chancellor, Lord Somers, and progressed rapidly due to her family connections. She was eight years older than Sir Joseph, and it was probably a political marriage connecting the two families. Lord Somers was much respected, and after his death in 1716 Sir Joseph inherited his large library and his wife Elizabeth his estate of Brookmans. Lord Somers' estate was divided between Elizabeth and her sister Mary Cocks, who inherited a house at Reigate, with other properties.

Most marriages of the time were arranged ones. They had no children, but Sir Joseph came from a large family. His father had married twice and it was through his half-brother Thomas that the Jekyll family descended. Thomas's elder son was a collector of customs at Boston, New England, while the younger married Anne, daughter of the Earl of Halifax, and their daughter Anne married George Wrighte of Gayhurst. Their son George died unmarried, while daughter Anne Barbara inherited the Hall.

A great-nephew Joseph was noted for his anti-slavery views, and his great-great-great-niece was Gertrude Jekyll, the landscape architect. One of his great-great-great-nephews was a friend of Robert Lewis Stephenson, and the name was used in *The Strange Case of Mr Jekyll and Mr Hyde*. He gave money to a friend for a colony to be founded on an island off the Georgia coast, named Jekyll island after him.

Sir Joseph was very active in parliament, speaking often, helping to draft bills and promote them. Though a Whig he often appeared to change his mind and did not always vote with the Whigs. He was against intoxication and supported Acts to increase the tax on gin, which annoyed the people so much there were riots and he had to have a guard outside his house. An unintended side effect was the production of illicit, and inferior, gin. At

Lincoln's Inn Fields he was once knocked down and almost killed, which led to the erection of pallisades and a garden. He wanted to become Lord Chancellor in 1725, and his failure made him Robert Walpole's enemy. He supported reform of the electoral system.

He was involved with the South Sea Company. In 1711 he was commissioner for subscriptions to the Company, and also held shares in the 1730s. Whether Jekyll had invested earlier, then sold before the crash in 1720, and whether this gave him the money to buy Dallington Hall, is another type of speculation. Alternatively he or his wife may have inherited money from Lord Somers.

The Company and the Bank of England (established 1694) were rivals in managing the Government national debt. The Company was started in 1711 ostensibly to trade with South America, but Spanish occupation prevented this. It was a time of many types of gambling, and buying shares or stock in a company was one form. Many joint stock companies were established, for all sorts of purposes, some fraudulent. The price of South Sea Company shares suddenly increased incredibly fast in 1720. This was a time of frenzied speculation, and the price of the shares rose from £128 in January 1720 to £1,000 in August, then collapsed in September to £175, ruining many investors. Sir Joseph convinced the government to investigate the collapse (the Bubble) in 1720. The Company became involved in slave trading, then arctic whaling, until 1763, afterwards managing Government debt until 1853.

Another Act he supported was to prevent the alienation (giving the title) of land to religious and charitable institutions. He was strongly anti-clerical and a patron of the freethinkers. Though generous to his relations he left his heir out of his will because the man returned from his travels through France and not Holland as Sir Joseph had ordered him.

He died in 1738 and was buried in the Rolls Chapel in Chancery Lane, London. In his will he left £20,000 of East India Stock for the reduction of the national debt. At the time this was around ten million pounds. From its beginnings politicians had intended to repay the debt, but never did. Elizabeth Jekyll died in 1745.

In 1747 an Act was passed to allow the sale of more of this stock for the benefit of his residual legatees, who were in want.

Several Jekylls lived in Dallington during the next century. One descendant was Joseph Jekyll Rye, Vicar of Dallington, a son of Sir Joseph's great niece Hannah who had married William Beauchamp Rye in 1751. This vicar gave many sermons away from Dallington, including at the Charterhouse chapel. Hannah had three sons and the second gave money for the almshouses. Hannah died at Bath in 1797. In 1819 Richard Jekyll Rye gave property 'by will' to the almshouses.

RESIDENTS

The earlier residents were enumerated in Samuel Sharpe's 1864 lecture to the Architectural Society. In the 1860s, the Spencer family of Althorp acquired the estate but rented it out. They bought and sold several small estates.

In both the 1841 and 1851 censuses John Reddall, Esquire and Magistrate, lived at Dallington Hall, with several indoor servants and a niece. After he died in 1856 the Hall was advertised for rent, unfurnished, from mid 1857.

The next tenant of Dallington Hall was Catherine Sharpe (nee Wheldon), daughter of a draper. She came from Stamford, Lincolnshire, and the 1841 census shows six 'pupils' living at her father's house there. This was typical of the small 'schools' in Victorian England, the sort of school the Brontë sisters attempted to start at Haworth.

In 1846 she married Samuel Sharpe of Uppingham, whose step-father owned and edited the *Stamford Mercury.* He studied geology and went to live near Northampton.

They opened a school for girls, Barn Hill House, Stamford, and in the 1851 census had sixteen resident pupils who came mostly from the local area between Lincoln and Northampton. In the 1851 census her name is given as Barbara Anne (a mistake by the enumerator?) and her parents lived with them. Interestingly, her father was born at Hardingstone.

They rented Dallington Hall, 'An Educational Establishment for Ladies' in 1857 with a 7-year lease. They advertised piano and harp, singing, English Literature, French, German, drawing and dancing, a curriculum that implies it was a finishing school, especially as most of the pupils were in their mid-teens.

A prospectus lists the charges. The basic charge was 32 guineas per annum, with extras charged at various rates:

> languages were six guineas each,
> harp eight per annum,
> dancing one pound two shillings per quarter,

use of books was three guineas per annum,
as also was a separate bed,
hot and cold baths appeared to be free.

In the 1861 census they had around fifty pupils.
These girls came from a wide area, their places of birth
including Somerset, Lancashire and Yorkshire, also
Ireland. A similar pattern is on the 1871 census.

The Sharpes had an adopted son, Samuel Henry
Jeyes, who won an open scholarship to Uppingham
school in 1869. In the 1861 census there were three
Jeyes nieces aged 11, 9 and 7 living with the Sharpes,
and by 1874 two of them were helping to run the school.
One taught drawing, the other literature. In 1869 Mr
Sharpe was selling cottages in Braunston and Helpstone,
which might possibly have belonged to the Jeyes family.

In 1876 during the Spring vacation they moved the
school to Great Harrowden Hall, near Wellingborough,
which by an odd coincidence had also been built around
1720. It is now a Golf Club. Mrs Sharpe advertised the
move in the Stamford Mercury, saying Lord Spencer
required Dallington for his own family, though the
Spencers did not in fact live at the Hall for some years.

This advertisement listed the offered curriculum.
There was singing, piano, organ and harmonium;
drawing and painting; English literature and language,
plus composition; French, German, Italian and Latin;
dancing and drilling. The girls played cricket, hockey and
tennis, and could ride and play golf. They had an
orchestra, and put on dramatic presentations. It is likely
many of these activities had also been available at
Dallington.

One of their pupils in 1889 was the last Queen of

the Hawaian royal family, Kaiulani, then aged fourteen, who reigned 1891-1893. She was deposed in 1893 and abdicated in 1895 and died three years later. One of her friends in Hawaii was Robert Lewis Stephenson who had gone there for his health.

Samuel died in 1886 at Great Harrowden Hall. Catherine retired to The Yews in Burton Latimer, where the Princess stayed with her in 1893.

The school closed in 1895 and Catherine died in 1907.

THE WHITWORTHS

Meanwhile Dallington Hall was rented by Mr Henry Whitworth, a banker, in 1877, but he died in December that year.

A novel, *Ready Money Mortiboy,* by Sir Walter Besant and James Rice, features Mr Whitworth. The heavily bearded Besant was a noted and prolific author of both fiction and non-fiction, while Rice, his collaborator for ten years until his death, was born in Northampton.

The agreement with Earl Spencer was for renting house, grounds and stabling. Water was to be pumped from the pond 'as now' through pipes, and the tenant was to keep pump and pipes in good repair.

Mrs Anne Whitworth, his widow, and an unmarried sister and niece stayed at Dallington Hall with four servants. The widow and niece were still there in 1891, with five servants.

In October 1888 there was a fire in the old part of the house, caused by soot in one of the big chimneys. A beam was also alight and there was a good deal of damage to paint and shutters. Two months later on

December 1st a known thief, Richard White, was caught trying to break into the house through the window of the china closet at 1.30am.

Mrs Whitworth died in September 1891.

THE SPENCERS

Members of the Spencer family lived at the Hall in later years. In 1901 there were five servants, plus Spencer children Delia (aged 11), Lavinia (aged 1) and Cecil, (aged 6). There were also a nursery maid, children's nurse, and governess.

In 1911, the last available census, the only inhabitants of the Hall were a caretaker, a widow Sarah Oram, aged 56, and a visitor with a daughter aged 1.

The Spencers at the Hall in 1901 were the children of Bobby and Margaret. In 1880 Bobby became a Whig MP at the age of twenty-two, the youngest MP at the time. He was noted for being exceptionally fashionably dressed, and his portraits show a heavy moustache.

Between 1880-1895 he represented North, then Mid Northants. In 1905 he was made a Viscount and went to the House of Lords as Lord Chamberlain. The House of Lords was described as a 'hospital for incurables'. He died in 1922.

Margaret was a member of the Baring banking family. She supported the Northampton Crippled Children's Fund and the Northampton Nursing Association, as well as the RSPCA.

Both she and Bobby were accomplished musicians, and frequently gave concerts in order to benefit local causes.

The family lived at the Hall for some time. Bobby

became the sixth Earl in 1910 and moved to Althorp in the following year. His wife had died in 1906 when giving birth to their sixth child at their London home in Bruton Street. Bobby was devastated, and never recovered.

HOSPITAL

Between 1915 to 1919 the house became a military hospital for about 80 beds, and 2,000 wounded passed through it. There is a picture of some of the injured soldiers playing croquet on the back lawn, and some of their graffiti remains on the courtyard wall.

The bare necessities were provided by the County, and an appeal was made in November 1915 for 'items of comfort', such as books, pictures and games. The first 25 patients were expected at the end of November. A grant of 3s (15p) per man per day would be given by the War Office and the balance provided by the County Red Cross Committee. Rev Streatfield, the local Vicar, offered his services as chaplain, and Dallington residents, having raised enough money to equip one bed, were planning to equip another.

There seemed to be plenty of entertainment for the soldiers. In January 1916 there was an entertainment by nurses from Weston Favell Hospital and friends, mainly of humourous sketches. In September during the annual fete Earl Spencer entertained 70 of the soldiers to tea at Althorp. In October 1916 a concert was held at the hospital and the girls working in Messrs Arnold and Sons, who collected money for gifts every week, gave cigarettes. On Christmas Day 1916 an autograph album designed by two of the soldiers, Lance-Corpl White and Private Wainer, and containing the signatures of patients and staff, was presented to Doctor Sanders along with a luminous wrist watch. Mrs Sanders was presented with a bouquet of pink carnations and roses.

A grant of £6,000 was received in April 1917 from the Central Demobilisation Board. The British Red Cross Society gave beds, bedding and other equipment valued at £1,500.

To celebrate the second anniversary of the

hospital's opening a whist drive was held in November 1917.

A soldier at the hospital, John Ferguson, was sued in September 1919 for maintenance of a child by Edith Spiers, who lived nearby. She was granted 2s 6d (12.5p) a week.

In 1919, in gratitude when both his sons survived the war, Earl Spencer gave the Hall and five acres of gardens to the people of Northampton for a convalescent home for twenty men and twenty women, with priority for disabled ex-servicemen and POWs.

The hospital was to become an annex of Northampton General Hospital, and in August 1920 work began. The condition of the roof and chimney stacks made it necessary to undertake more repairs than had been planned, but the convalescent home for 20 men and 20 women was opened in December that year by Earl Spencer, who asked that it be named the Margaret Spencer Home of Rest in memory of his wife. A picture of the late Viscountess was presented by the Dallington Musical Competition Choir, which she had conducted from 1899 to 1905.

The home was of great benefit to the town. In one year, 1923, 596 patients had been admitted, 283 male, 313 female, and on average they stayed for 19 days. Some were cured, other transferred back to the hospital or to other convalescent homes. By 1943 it had been decided the home would cater for women only, as a new home for male patients had been opened in Spratton.

A fete was held at the home in August 1924, and on Christmas Day that year the Mayor and Mayoress visited.

A gift of radios was made by the Merry Comrades

in 1948. They had previously installed them in the General Hospital. This charity had begun in 1911 as a newspaper column for children, then developed into a fund-raising charity.

The stables, which had accommodated male patients, were adapted in 1948 for nurses, and wiring and an electronic call system installed. In 1979 planning permission was granted for the convalescent home to be converted to a private hospital, the Margaret Spencer Hospital, but this did not appear to have been done. Instead the Home was closed with the approval of the Secretary of State for Social Services despite the recommendation of the local community health council.

CONSERVATION

In 1969 Northampton Borough Council listed the building as grade 2* and in 1970 Dallington was designated a conservation area. By the Church is the Queen's Recreation Ground, now a car park, presented to the village by the fifth Earl in 1897 to commemorate Queen Victoria's 60 years on the throne. In 1970 permission was given for the house to be converted into a house and four self-contained flats. Later the empty property was badly vandalised, almost every window being broken.

In the 1980s Roger Pinnock came to the rescue by converting the house into apartments. Roger started as an accountant at GEC in Rugby, but he helped found a squash club in the tennis club premises, opposite the Hall.

Pinnock and a friend, architect Daniel Xielinski, became partners in the firm of Craigside and successfully converted Gayhurst House, north of Milton Keynes, into apartments.

Daniel built modern homes in the SE part of the grounds of Dallington Hall, while Roger converted part of the house into four (later five) apartments. Some ceilings were lowered, and rooms divided.

The stable block had four more homes and there was a bachelor flat over the archway entrance. The hedges were planted at this time. In 1989 permission was granted for 'a pair of stone piers with wrought iron gates', but this does not appear to have been done. Instead iron pillars have been installed, with the gates.

Outside Raynsford Road (part of it renamed Dallington Park Road) was busy, but the new road, Mill Lane, completed soon afterwards, took away this traffic. It also split the tennis club. Before this road was completed the only direct access to Kingsthorpe was via a very muddy track beyond Heathville.

One of the first residents to move into the new apartments was Robert Spencer, grandson of Bobby, the sixth Earl. His father had been George, Bobby's youngest son. Robert was a bachelor who had lived at Langton Hall in Leicestershire. He took what is now the Hall, saying Langton was too big for him. He had electricity installed, driven by a water wheel. Presumably mains electricity had been cut off when the convalescent home moved out.

DALLINGTON PARK

Dallington Park, the old warren, which is adjacent to Dallington Hall, is 23 acres. When the sixth Earl Spencer decided to auction it in 1920 the three brothers, Charles, Edward and Thomas Lewis, shoe manufacturers who

lived in The Avenue and Harlestone Road, and whose factory, the St James Works, was at the end of Dallington Road on the corner of Vicarage Road, offered to buy it and give it to the town.

The Council had been negotiating with the Earl's agent and agreed a price. Councillor Edward wrote to the Council that

> 'It would afford my brothers (Mr Charles Lewis and Councillor T.D.Lewis) and myself great pleasure to provide the agreed purchase price of the Park as a gift to the town if the Council will accept it. The Corporation would, of course, undertake to utilise the Park as one of the open spaces or recreation grounds of Northampton.'

The Council gratefully accepted the offer.

For some years the Dallington & District Horticultural Society held their annual show in the Park each August. This Society had begun in the 1860s, and some previous shows had been held in the Lotus Sports Ground. It had for a time also been a horse show. The annual show had been 'a bit dodgy' for thirty years, but

37

was resurrected in 1943 at the racecourse, then was moved to the Park where it was held each year until 1958. The tenant, a Mr Spurgin, and Earl Spencer had been agreeable. People like Tom Forrest of *The Archers* and Freddy Grisewood, a broadcaster perhaps best known for being the host of *Any Questions?* from its beginning in 1948 until 1967, came to open it officially. There was a big marquee, the usual competitions for vegetables, fruit, flowers, jam, cakes, eggs, honey and so on as well as various handicrafts. There were demonstrations, for example on bee-keeping, music from the Rushton Temperance Band, bowling for a pig, sideshows, sales, tea and ices. There were also walks round the ponds, with tennis club grounds open to visitors and the trees decked with fairy lights.

Today the Park is well used. Joggers and dog walkers are there every day, and in fine weather the children's playground is well patronized. Football or cricket matches take place at weekends. The Friends of Dallington Park have constructed a small garden.

Lewis Brothers' Factory (Grace's guide to British Industry 1919)

The Lewis brothers were late comers to the Northampton shoe industry. Their father had arrived from Wales and died leaving £27. His sons left £200,000. They built their large four-storey factory on a green field site. It no longer exists, but Lewis Road, leading to it from Warren Road, remembers the brothers.

Thomas Davis Lewis was a trustee of the Almshouses, appointed in 1927 by Northampton Borough Council. He left the sum of £1,000 for the provision of a scholarship or scholarships for educational purposes in the County of Northampton. His daughter, Margaret Lewis, gave to the trustees an additional payment for further scholarships. It now provides both undergraduate and postgraduate students with financial awards of up to £1,500. This scholarship is awarded on educational excellence or potential.

CONCLUSION

There are still many questions, such as why Sir Joseph chose to build in Dallington, whether he ever lived in the Hall, when the Dower House extension was added, when and why the closed two-storey passageway between the main house and the gatehouse was built. Who was the architect? Was it Francis Smith who built Lamport Rectory, and is thought to have been involved in the building of Great Harrowden Hall?

Dallington was a small manor whose owners had many connections to national government, far more than in comparable villages.

Dallington Hall was a small house, compared with others built around the same time, such as Lydiard House and Acton Round House (another Smith design), and especially Blenheim. It was not Sir Joseph's main house, which was Brookmans, larger and closer to London, so did he spend much time here? Given that so many Jeyklls lived in Dallington in the next few decades, had he perhaps built it to provide for his large family of nephews and nieces? He was 58 in 1720, and might not have expected to live much beyond the completion date ten years later. He had twelve siblings, at least half of them still alive in 1720, and some of the others having had children. Many of the wider Jekyll family lived in Dallington in the next century.

Over the past three hundred years the Hall has undergone many changes, served many different functions, and is now the home of eleven families. In 2020 we are celebrating its history.

***